FOLENS

GW01464500

IDEAS BANK

THE INDUS VALLEY

a past non-European society

Jill Bennett

Contents

+ book review for those not done

Folens Publishers

How to use this book

Ideas Bank books provide ready to use, practical, photocopiable activity pages for children, **plus** a wealth of ideas for extension and development.

TEACHER IDEAS PAGE

PHOTOCOPIABLE ACTIVITY PAGE

Clear focus to the activity.

Suggestions for developing work on the photocopiable pages.

Extension activities suggested to take the work one stage further.

Independent activities for children to work with.

- Time-saving, relevant and practical, **Ideas Bank** books ensure that you will always have work ready to hand.

Jill Bennett would like to acknowledge the valuable assistance given by Vikram Singh in the research for this project in India.

Editor: Andy Brown   Layout artist: Patricia Hollingsworth

Cover by: In Touch Creative Services Ltd.   Illustrations by: Jeffrey Burn – Graham-Cameron Illustration

First published 1995 by Folens Limited, Albert House, Apex Business Centre, Boscombe Road, Dunstable, LU5 4RL, England.

ISBN 1 85276641 7

Printed in Singapore by Craft Print

Introduction

The Indus Valley civilisation was one of the world's first four 'great' civilisations. Its cities were thriving some 4000 years ago and were contemporary with the ancient cities in Egypt and Mesopotamia. The civilisation is thought to have come into existence over 4500 years ago and was at its height between 2500 and 2000BC. Although not the oldest of the ancient civilisations, the Indus Valley civilisation does appear to have been the most extensive, stretching roughly a thousand miles from its northernmost settlements in what is now Pakistan to its southernmost sites in what is now Gujarat (in India).

In spite of its size, comparatively little is known about the Indus Valley civilisation and many questions remain unanswered. However, in recent years considerable progress has been made in solving some of the mysteries of the Indus cities by the joint efforts of archaeologists from India, Pakistan, the USA, Britain and some other European countries.

Almost all of our knowledge of the Indus Valley civilisation is based on archaeological evidence. A study of this civilisation should help to develop the children's knowledge and understanding of archaeology in general as well as helping them develop some understanding of the Indus civilisation itself.

There are many kinds of archaeological investigation. It is often necessary to dig into the ground in search of evidence of how people lived in the past. However, this excavating is only one small aspect of archaeology. Much of the work is done after the digging, when experts of various kinds examine what has been found. Children need to be made aware of this.

Archaeology offers suggestions on how people lived in the past and allows us to make comparisons with our own lives today. We may sometimes find that not all developments can be thought of as 'progress'. For example, it seems that the citizens of the Indus Valley civilisation managed to maintain a peaceful society over a wide area for a long period of time without a large army. Today, even small nations spend vast sums of money on defence.

Archaeology also shows that many of the 'poorer' countries by today's standards – those which people of the more affluent first world countries may view as inferior – were once the homes of great, thriving civilisations.

The main factor hindering progress in solving the remaining mysteries of the Indus Valley civilisation is the lack of written evidence. Although over 2000 inscriptions have been found, mainly on seals, most of these bear only a few characters; no written records of any length have been found. From the evidence we have it seems that:

- The Indus Valley citizens had developed their own script which used pictographic signs.
- The small seals bearing inscriptions were probably used for commercial purposes as a means of identifying goods.
- Longer records may have been kept on perishable materials such as cloth, wood or even palm leaves.

The demise of the Indus Valley civilisation is another of the unsolved mysteries. At one time it was thought that invading Indo-Aryans were responsible, but contemporary thinking has now changed from 'who' to 'what' caused the decline and ultimate abandonment of the great cities:

"Just as the creation and maintenance of the system was the outcome of the successful combination of several factors, so too its breakdown could have been caused by the weakening of any one of these or the upsetting of their harmonious balance and interaction." (Allchin, B and R, *The Rise of Civilisation in India and Pakistan*, CUP 1982.)

These authors cite suggestions other historians have made which include:

- a decline in the rainfall leading to a decrease in agricultural output in regions through which trade caravans passed
- wearing out of the land due to over-cultivation
- a period of major tectonic disturbance (the whole region lies in a major earthquake zone)
- changes in the course of rivers resulting in desiccation of agricultural lands
- flooding
- epidemic diseases.

All we can be sure of is that the Indus urban phase did come to an end.

This book includes illustrations that are intended to represent the Indus peoples. As there is insufficient historical evidence to give clues to their appearence, we must emphasise that these are merely an artist's impression of how the Indus peoples may have looked.

Aim

- To give children an understanding of the chronology of the Indus Valley civilisation in relation to those of the Egyptian and Mesopotamian civilisations.

Background

India's most ancient cities and towns were thriving over 4000 years ago. The ancient civilisations of Egypt and Mesopotamia were their contemporaries. These, like the Indus Valley civilisation, were located along great rivers. Of the three, the Indus civilisation seems to have been the most extensive geographically, stretching over 1000 miles north to south. Ancient Egypt and Mesopotamia are well-researched and chronicled but relatively little is known about the Indus civilisation, specific events in its history or individuals.

Gold beads and pendants of Mesopotamian origin were found in a merchant's house at Lothal and etched carnelian beads and long-barrel beads of Harappan origin have been found at Kish and Ur in Mesopotamia. Much imported pottery from this period has been found at Lothal as well as terracotta models of Egyptian mummies.

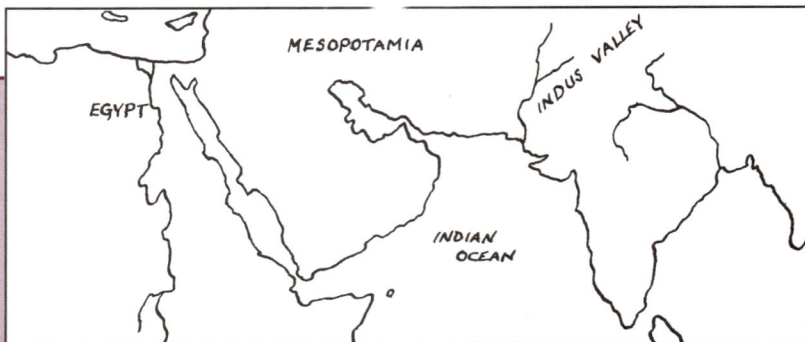

Activity Sheet

- Ask the children to study the time line. Draw their attention to the fact that all three civilisations overlapped in time.
- The children could write each of the statements in the appropriate place on the time line.
- Time lines could be displayed and the chronology of the three civilisations discussed.
- Ask the children to find out what was happening in their own country at this time. What conclusions can they draw?

Developments

- Children could look at an historical atlas and locate the ancient Egyptian and Mesopotamian civilisations. How might traders from Lothal have reached these places?
- Archaeologists have found Mesopotamian seals at Indus sites and Indus seals in Mesopotamian cities. What do the children think this suggests about contact between the two regions? Copy and complete the chart below. Use a similar chart for other investigations.

Evidence	Conclusion
Seals from Mesopotamia found at Harappa. Indus seals found in Ur.	

- Persian Gulf seals of Bahrein origin have been found at Lothal and in some Mesopotamian cities. Do the children think settlements on the Persian Gulf played any part in the trade – if so, what?

IDEAS BANK – *The Indus Valley*

Time line of ancient civilisations

- Read the statements about the history of three ancient civilisations.
  Write each one in the correct place on the time line.

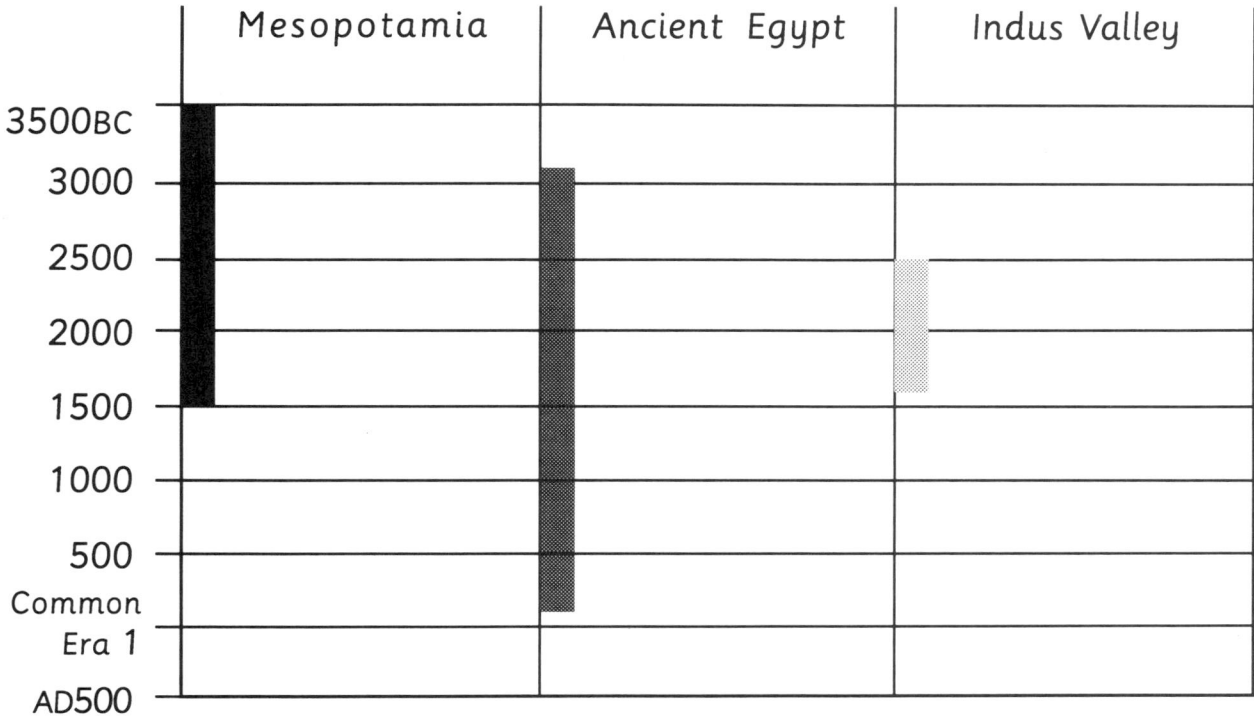

	Mesopotamia	Ancient Egypt	Indus Valley
3500BC			
3000			
2500			
2000			
1500			
1000			
500			
Common Era 1			
AD500			

2577–2134BC   –   Pyramids built at Giza

2350BC   –   Indus settlers build town and dock at Lothal

2000BC   –   Ur (Mesopotamia) sacked by invaders

2200–2000BC   –   Lothal trades with Egypt and Sumeria

3000BC   –   Development of hieroglyphs

3500BC   –   Writing invented. The oldest inscribed tablet from Kish (Mesopotamia 3100BC)

1900BC   –   Great flood – Lothal razed to the ground

2500BC   –   King Sargon conquers all Mesopotamia

1500BC   –   Mesopotamian and Egyptian kings trade riches (Tutankhamun and Rameses II are kings)

332BC   –   Alexander conquers Egypt. Persians no longer rule

Aims

- To introduce knowledge and understanding of the area of the Indus Valley civilisation.
- To enable children to locate the sites of the most important cities and towns of the Indus civilisation.

Background

The Indian sub-continent is the home of the Indus Valley civilisation, one of the world's four great ancient civilisations. It came into existence about 4500 years ago along the valley of the River Indus and spread to many sites over a vast area covering more than 1 000 000 square miles of land in what is now India and Pakistan. The discovery of the sites of the cities of Mohenjo-daro, Harappa and Chanhu-daro in Pakistan, as well as Lothal and Kalibangan in India, have resulted in some important archaeological findings.

Map showing PAKISTAN, R. INDUS, DELHI, KARACHI, INDIA, INDIAN OCEAN

KEY
- ⋯⋯⋯ River valley
- ∿∿∿ Country border
- ∼∼∼ River

Activity Sheet

- Use world maps to:
  – locate the study area
  – relate the children's locality in terms of direction and distance.
- What are the names of the Indus cities and towns marked on the map? An historical atlas may be necessary.
- In which countries are the sites now?

A view of the Indus city of Mohenjo-daro today.

Developments

- Locate the Indus sites in relation to modern towns or cities.
- Have any of the children visited the area? They could be invited to recount some of their experiences.
- What problems might distance have caused for communication and trade in the time of the Indus Valley civilisation?
- Using an atlas, work out possible trade routes with the other contemporary civilisations, such as Mesopotamia and Egypt.
- The children could calculate distances between Indus sites, for example, Lothal and Mohenjo-daro. They could speculate on how long the journey might have taken and what means of transport would have been used at the time. They should list the evidence they would need to be able to answer such questions. How would travelling then have been different from making the same journey today?

Site 1	Site 2	Distance	Transport
Mohenjo – daro	Harappa	475 km	Donkey and cart ?

The Indus Valley civilisation

- Label the sites of the main Indus Valley cities and towns.
- Use an atlas and label: a) the Thar Desert   b) the Arabian Sea
                           c) the Aravalli Mountains d) the River Indus
                           e) the River Sabarmati.

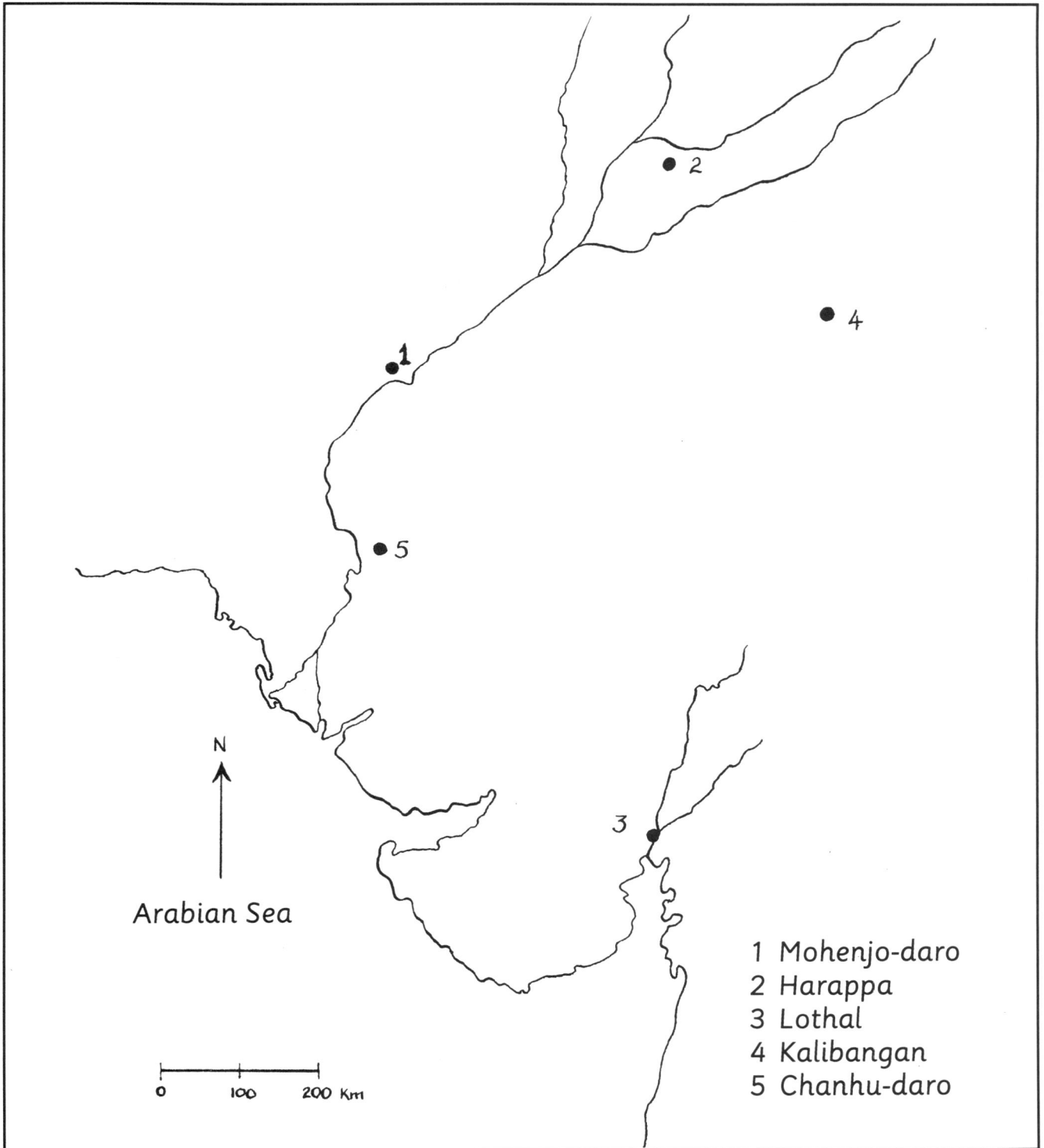

● 2

● 4

● 1

● 5

N

Arabian Sea

3 ●

0   100   200 Km

1 Mohenjo-daro
2 Harappa
3 Lothal
4 Kalibangan
5 Chanhu-daro

© Folens

IDEAS BANK – The Indus Valley

7

What is a civilisation? –

Aims

- To consider what is meant by a civilisation.
- To look generally at reasons why civilisations develop.
- To consider why and how civilisation developed in the Indus region.

Activity Sheet

- Ask the children to think about their nearest town or city and to suggest what elements make it a civilised community. Copy and complete the chart.

Town or city	What makes it 'civilised'?
London	Many roads. Railways. Shopping centres. Hospitals. Government.

- Working in pairs or small groups, the children could read and discuss the information given.
- They should then match up the statements and discuss any conclusions to be drawn.
  Answers: A1 / B5 / C2 / D4 / E3

Background

The activity sheet gives the main factors common to the development of a civilisation and information about the Indus sites which are evidence of that civilisation.

Archaeologists have pinpointed some key occurences in the civilisation, even though little was written at the time. The Harappans arrived at Lothal, a small settlement, around 2400BC and developed and expanded the town.

A dock was planned and built around 2350BC after a flood had washed away much of the pre-existing village. The Harappans were attracted to Lothal by its bead-making industry and they developed and expanded its industry and trading of the finished products during the period 2200–2000BC.

For all their prosperity the Indus people were unable to cope with repeated severe flooding. Around 1900BC another great flood swept away Lothal and it was never to be rebuilt.

Developments

- Ask the groups to imagine that their town was totally abandoned. Buildings and their contents remained intact except that all paper and cloth had turned to dust. How would an explorer from another galaxy know that civilisation had existed?
- Can they construct evidence for civilisation and match it to the same developments on the sheet? A different way of displaying this information is by writing it on a circular diagram and matching the statements to the correct picture by turning the circle.
- Ask the children to consider the level of skill and the extent of technology required to develop some of the aspects of this 'civilised' society. Are they surprised? Why?

Evidence	Skills required	Technology
Bricks all the same size and shape	Clay making, shaping, firing	Kilns

What is a civilisation?

● Match the labels A–E with the correct pictures 1–5.

A
Advances in building, technology and mathematics.

B
Accurate systems of weights and measures develop.

C
Some goods are traded. People travel to trade.

D
Some people specialise in crafts.

E
People start to keep records and write.

1
Streets built in a grid pattern. Buildings carefully designed and built.

2
Indus seals found in Mesopotamia. Warehouse and dock at Lothal.

3
Over 2500 inscriptions found, mainly on seals.

4
Highly specialised crafts, such as shell working and inlaying, pottery, bead-making, stone-blade making.

5
Uniform systems of weight and measures.

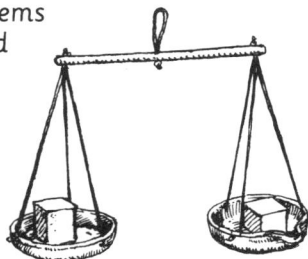

Finding out about the past – Ideas Page

Aims

- To introduce the process of making deductions and forming hypotheses using the evidence available as basic principles in archaeology.
- To give the children experience in making deductions and forming hypotheses from artefacts.

Activity Sheet

- Play the 'Mystery object' game. Give pairs of children a 'mystery object' and an activity sheet. They should record each idea or fact on their chart. You may want to ask for a 'report' on the findings at the end of the session.
- Suggested mystery objects might include: a diva lamp, an incense holder, a shoe horn, a button hook, a lemon squeezer.
- Discuss how this activity reflects the problems of dealing with archaeological evidence.

Incense holder

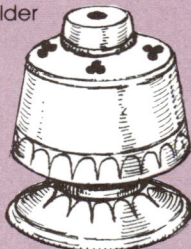

Diva lamp

Background

Archaeology is a study of the human past, using a variety of evidence left by the people of the past such as:

- Material remains or objects. Archaeologists may study ancient buildings, monuments, artefacts such as pottery, tools and implements, images or coins.
- Geographical traces – field systems, for instance, may be studied.
- Scientifically-discovered traces such as deposits of pollen from crops. Thus, modern archaeology is a combination of history, geography, anthropology and religious studies with science and technology. It may depend upon the latest developments in these subjects, for example radio-carbon dating.

Rather than furnishing indisputable facts, archaeological investigations allow archaeologists to interpret the past, or rather 'a past', by using the information available at that particular time. Any such interpretation based on available evidence may subsequently be proved unsatisfactory by future discoveries which furnish conflicting evidence.

This has happened with many of the theories relating to the Indus Valley civilisation, where new evidence and the discovery of new sites has cast doubt on theories about the origins and development of the civilisation and its decline.

Developments

- Fill a small holdall with a variety of objects. The children should pretend it has been found and taken to a lost property office. In small groups ask them to reconstruct the life of the person who lost it. What can they be sure about? What may be true? Children could record their thoughts and findings in a chart.

Object	What we can be sure about	What may be true?	Evidence
A teddy bear	Its shape, size, colour, weight, what it is made from	It is a toy. It is looked after	We have seen other toys like it. It is not damaged

- One member of the group can choose a range of favourite possessions to be buried with. The other group members try to decide what would remain in 500 years' time and what the remains might tell about the person.

Be an archaeologist

● Work in pairs. Write in the spaces about your mystery object.

What do we know?	What do we think possible?

MYSTERY OBJECT:

What is the evidence?	What do we need to find out?

● What have you learned about the problems an archaeologist faces?

Aim

- To show how archaeological discoveries can very often involve piecing together evidence from different people, over many years.

Activity Sheet

- Read the background information to the children. Ask them to imagine they are Sir John Marshall. They could write a report for the *Illustrated London News* about the discovery of the Indus civilisation. They should include an illustration with an appropriate caption and invent a headline.

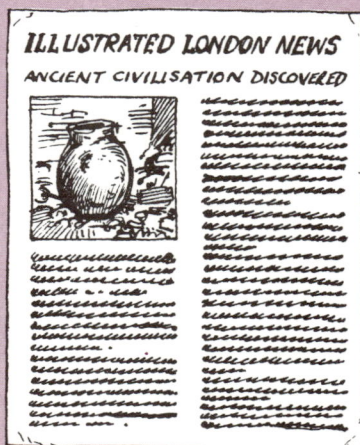

ILLUSTRATED LONDON NEWS
ANCIENT CIVILISATION DISCOVERED

Background

An English traveller, Charles Mason, was possibly the first to visit Harappa in 1826. He described the 'ruinous brick castle' and 'the remarkably high walls and towers'.

In 1831, Alexander Burns was impressed by the extensive ruins and estimated them to be about three miles in circumference. Both men had been told by local people about a great city that had been in existence there long ago, a city which, they said, was destroyed by God in anger at the misdeeds of the ruling king.

Alexander Cunningham, first Archaeological Surveyor of India, carried out investigations of the site between 1853 and 1873. He thought that Harappa may have been the site of a Greek settlement but found nothing to confirm this. He did, however, draw a site plan and find some artefacts including a seal.

In 1920, Rakhal Das Banerji excavated a Buddhist stupa built on one of the mounds and discovered several layers considerably older beneath it. He also found a number of objects including some seals. A link between Mohenjo-daro and Harappa was established.

Sir John Marshall, Director General of the Archaeological Survey of India, realised the significance of the discoveries and in 1924 compared the finds from Mohenjo-daro with those from Harappa. He concluded that these objects had a common origin and were different from anything previously known in India.

Developments

- Write reports from the different points of view of the different archaeologists who visited the sites.
- The children could write letters to the *Illustrated London News* giving explanations for what was found, based on the evidence.
- They could discuss how and why the civilisation remained hidden so long to western people.
- What does the story tell us about the difficulty of interpreting evidence?

Press report

- Imagine that you are Sir John Marshall and that you have just returned from India. Write a report about your discoveries for the Illustrated London News. It should include an illustration (with a caption) and a headline.

ILLUSTRATED LONDON NEWS

Aim

- To demonstrate that archaeologists often make deductions from partial or incomplete information.

Background

The Great Bath at Mohenjo-daro was 12 metres long, 7 metres wide and 3 metres deep. At the north and south end, steps (originally covered by wooden treads), led down to the floor of the tank. To make it waterproof, there was a layer of pitch sandwiched between the inner and outer layer of the Bath's brick skins. The Bath was filled with water drawn from a well in one of the rooms adjacent to the courtyard. It obviously played a part in the civic-religious life of the community, but its real significance is unknown. Archaeologists have concluded that it may have been used for some kind of communal religious ritual.

Activity Sheet

- Ask the children to cut out and study the pieces of the Bath.
- They should make the entire picture by using the 'evidence' they can see.
- The children could paste the pieces on to a larger sheet of paper and label anything they can see. They should research the features they are unsure of.

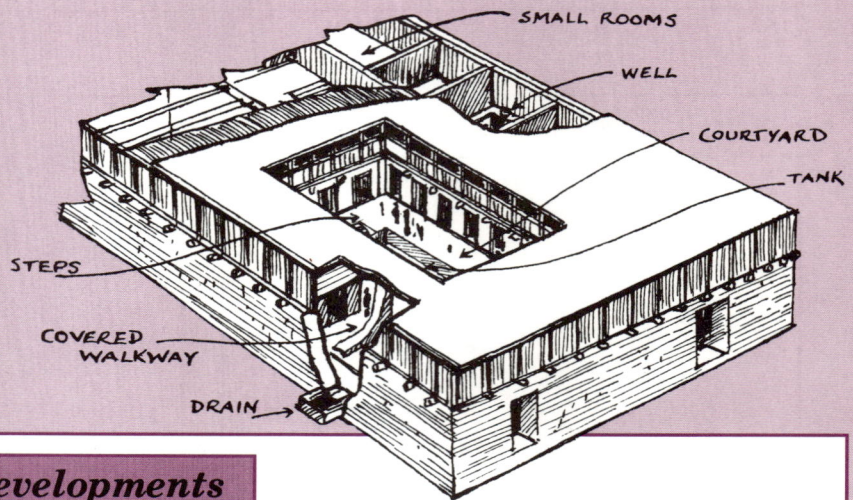

Developments

- Groups could compare their picture and their labels.
- Give the children a list of questions archaeologists have asked about buildings such as the Great Bath:
  - Why are some buildings built on a platform?
  - Why were brick containers near the Great Bath full of animal bones?
  - Why was there a series of shallow pits containing ashes and charcoal near to the Bath?
- Ask them to consider interpretations and the evidence for them.

Mystery	Interpretation	Evidence
Pits with ashes.	Sacrifices of animals for religious purposes.	Charcoal, ashes, animal bones, near a large building.

- Children should compare their interpretations and discusss the kinds of evidence they would need to be sure of their deductions.
- Challenge them to find out about religious groups today that use rituals involving bathing.

The Great Bath at Mohenjo-daro

● Look carefully at the pieces. Cut them out and put them together using any evidence you can find to help you.

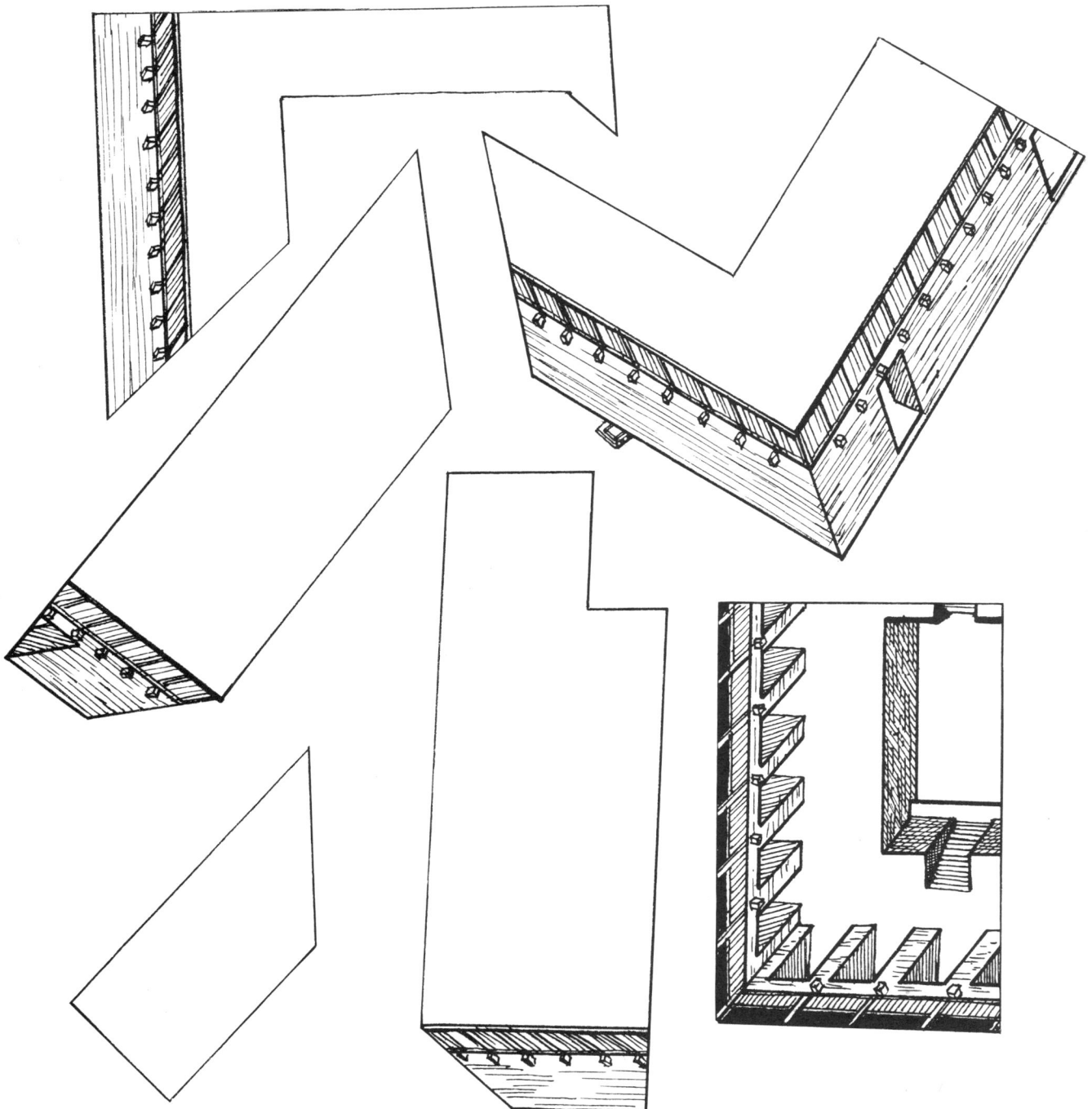

What problems do archaeologists face when they try to piece together a picture of the past?

Lothal 1 – Ideas Page

Aims

- To develop knowledge and understanding of the layout and construction of Lothal.
- To relate features in the picture to those shown on the plan (page 19).
- To alert children to the measures taken in the construction of Lothal to counter the problems of flooding.

Activity Sheet

- Discuss the background information with the children.
- Ask them to look at the artist's impression of Lothal and to identify some of the features.
- Ask what evidence the artist needed to draw an accurate picture of Lothal.
- Why should historians be suspicious of artists' impressions?

Example of Indus drainage system (Mohenjo-daro).

Background

The town planners of Lothal made the town safe from flooding, by building houses on terraced platforms. The whole town was enclosed within a 13-metre-thick wall for additional protection. Like other Indus cities, Lothal was divided into two parts: the acropolis, where the 'ruler' and his associates lived; and the lower town. (Information on the acropolis is given on page 18.)

The lower town contained the main street, lined with shops, which was the commercial centre, where the rich merchants and the craftsmen lived. The residential part of the town lay to the east and west of this street. Residential buildings, small coppersmiths' and bead makers' workshops were built in straight rows on either side of the main street.

There was a dock for ships on the eastern side of the town. According to modern oceanography experts 'the construction of a dock ... near the mouth of the River Sabaramati ... points to the fact that the Harappans possessed a high degree of knowledge relating to ebb and flow tides ...'.

There was also a warehouse, used for examining and storing cargo. It was built near the citadel on a 3.5m high mud platform and covered an area of 48.7 x 39.6 metres. **Information on the acropolis is given on page 18.**

A reconstruction of an Indus house found at Mohenjo-daro.

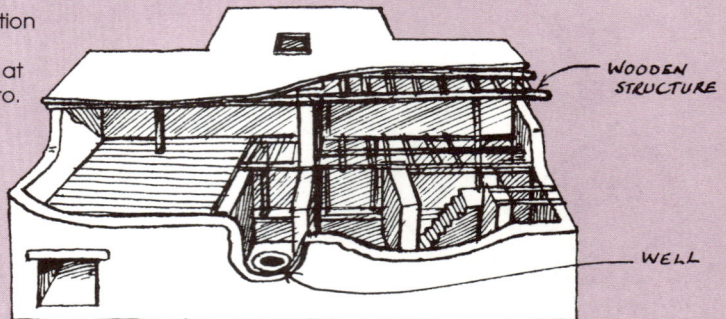

WOODEN STRUCTURE

WELL

Developments

- The children could relate the picture to the map on page 16 and identify the features.
- Discuss why they think there was a wall around Lothal. Why were the buildings built on platforms of bricks?
- Consider some of the consequences of a rise in the level of the River Indus.

What happens to the Indus	Consequence
River floods	Brings fertile soil to the valley. Good agriculture. Too much water could destroy the fields and ruin the crops.
River floods	Towns could be destroyed, people killed
River does not flood	No rich soil. Not enough food grown.

IDEAS BANK – *The Indus Valley*

Lothal

- Look at how one artist imagined Lothal.
- Label it with these features:

– the warehouse	– streets	– drains
– the acropolis	– the wharf	– the outer wall
– the dock	– the entrance to the town	– houses

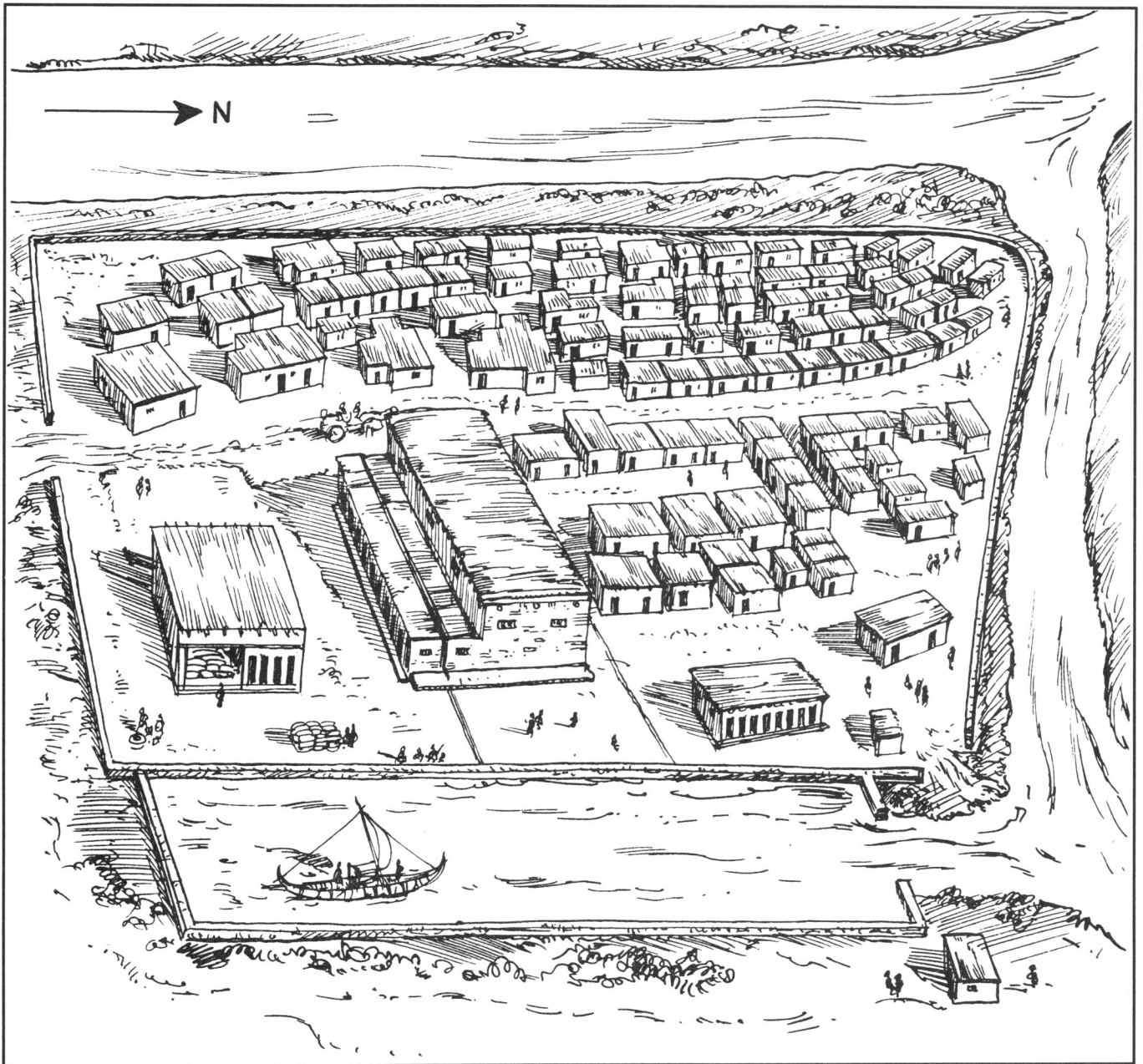

Compare Lothal with where you live. How is it different?
How is it the same?

Aims

- To give children an idea of the layout of the town of Lothal.
- To introduce the various buildings (warehouse, bead factory, dwellings, smithy and acropolis) and structures (town wall, dock, drains, kilns, wells and cesspools).
- To give children a concept of the size of a town (the excavated site measures 284.6m north to south and 228m east to west). At the height of its prosperity it is thought to have covered a wider area, as indicated by habitation remains 300m south of the present mound.

Background

The raised platform in Lothal on which the acropolis stood measured 127.4 metres from east to west and 60.9 metres north to south. The plan view on the activity sheet is based on archaeologists' drawings. It shows the acropolis as a single building. In fact, it was a collection of many houses, including that of the ruler of Lothal, which was made from kiln-fired bricks.

At the southern edge of the acropolis, 12 baths were built in a straight row with outlet channels that joined up with the main underground sewer. The construction of the baths was of high quality: the bricks were polished to give fine joints and to prevent water seepage.

Other houses in the acropolis also had paved baths, underground drains and a well. The drains suggest that, inside the acropolis area, there were three streets and two lanes that ran east to west and two streets that ran north to south.

There was yet another row of houses to the north of the acropolis. These had small baths which connected to a second underground sewer.

The whole city was kept clean by a network of drains, manholes and cesspools. The main sewers, joined by small channels, emptied waste into the dock to be washed away at high tide.

Information on the lower town is given on page 16.

Activity Sheet

- Ask the children to make a key using the activity sheet on page 17.
- Challenge the children to work out the approximate length of the wall around the town. Also, ask them to measure the warehouse and/or the citadel (acropolis).

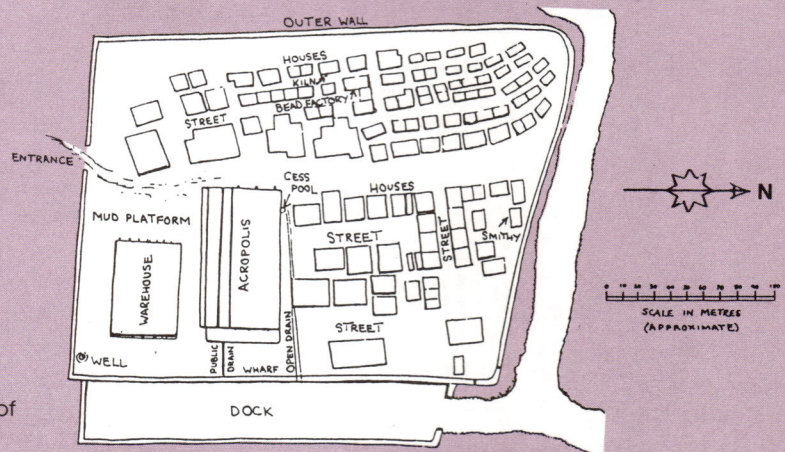

How an Indus building may have looked.

A map of Lothal.

Developments

- The streets tend to be of a similar width, run in straight lines and follow a grid pattern. What does this suggest? What conclusions could be drawn from these deductions?

Evidence	Deductions	Conclusions
Straight roads in a grid pattern.	Built by engineers? Planned? People used maths?	There must have been some form of building regulations enforced by those who ruled.

A plan view of Lothal

- Using the plan below and the activity sheet 'Lothal', make a key of the town of Lothal, using a different colour for each thing on the key.

N

KEY

warehouse	
acropolis	
dock	
town entrance	
wharf	
drains	
outer wall	
houses	

0 10 20 30 40 50 60 70 80 90 100

SCALE IN METRES
(APPROXIMATE)

NOW Colour the plan according to the key you have made.

Indus weight systems –

Aims

- To appreciate the accuracy and uniformity of the Indus weight system.
- To help children appreciate the difficulties of constructing a uniform weight system.

Activity Sheet

- Ask the children to calculate the weight for each ratio. (The 27.584g weight has been rounded up to 28g for ease of calculation.)
- Provide modelling clay and kitchen scales for them to make the weights. They should decide:
  – which weights they need to make
  – how many of each will be needed.
- The children will find that it is not possible to construct a set of weights that are exactly equivalent to 500g, although they can get very close to it (498.8g).
- Once the first set of weights have been made, can the children replicate the weights accurately using a balance, not scales?

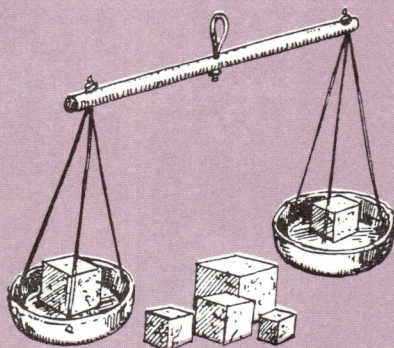

Background

The Indus citizens manufactured weights at several centres, including Lothal. These were made from agate and fine-grained chert. The accuracy and uniformity of the Indus weights has few parallels in history and is especially significant when we consider the huge area that the Indus civilisation covered. The characteristic stone weights were hexahedron shaped, in contrast to those of the Ancient Egyptians which were 'duck shaped' and those of the Sumerians which were barrel shaped. The Indus citizens used these weights for purposes of foreign trade. The craftsmen who made them blunted the edges before polishing them to ensure their accuracy and uniformity. There were three weight systems.

The unit weight for weighing commodities of daily use, such as fruits or grain, was 27.584g and ran in the ratio 0.05, 0.1, 0.2, 0.5, 2, 5, 10, 20, 50, 100, 200, 500.

The lowest basic weight system was used for weighing precious stones, metals and pearls. It consisted of small gold discs of 50mg, 100mg, 200mg through to 3250mg.

A third series had the smallest weight as 0.871g and ran in the ratio 0.05, 0.1, 0.2, 0.5, 1, 2 and 10

Developments

- Organise a role-play of a market scene using the weights. What would the people be selling and buying? How could this be discovered by archaeologists?
- Did the children encounter difficulties when calculating the ratios? If so, what does the existence of such a sophisticated weight system prove about the people of the Indus valley? Copy and complete the chart.

Evidence	My idea
Weights found	They used a mathematical system
Different weights for different things	

- The children could research the weight systems of other ancient societies and compare them to their own.

	Egypt	Mesopotamia	Indus Valley	Today
Shape ?				
Made from ?				
Weight ?				
Used for ?				

Indus weight systems

Everyday weights were found with the ratios listed in the table below. The unit weight was about 28g.

Can you make a set of weights for a Lothal market trader to weigh out goods up to 500g?

- What weights will you need to make?
- How many of each weight will you need?

Use the table to help you. You could use a calculator to help.

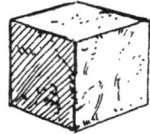

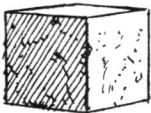

INDUS WEIGHT SYSTEM FOR A MARKET TRADER		
Ratio	Weight in gms	Number to be made
0.05		
0.1		
0.2		
0.5		
1	28g	
2		
5		
10		
20		
50		
100		
200		
500		

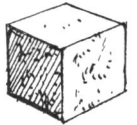

Ceramic art – Ideas Page

Aims

- To introduce knowledge about Indus Valley ceramic art.
- To demonstrate a possible link between the Indus Valley culture and that of the Ancient Greeks.

Background

For thousands of years people have enjoyed telling stories about animals. Probably the most well-known are Aesop's fables which date from around 600BC. But these are thought to be retellings of even earlier stories. There are stories featuring many of the same animals in the Sanskrit literature of the Panchatantra, an Indian 'Book of Knowledge'.

Before the stories were written down, people used word of mouth and pictures. Some of the earthenware jars found at Lothal are decorated with narrative paintings of animals that have many similarities with those we know in Aesop's fables.

Below is an historian's description of one of the red ware jars found at Lothal:

The vessel surface was divided into horizontal and vertical panels. The colour scheme was black on a red surface or chocolate on a buff surface. The Lothal artist introduced realism. He showed animals in their natural surroundings. His most important contribution is the narrative style. On a large vessel the artist has depicted birds perched on a tree holding fish in a beak. At the foot of the tree is a fox-like animal with a stumpy tail and a fish has fallen down. This reminds us of the story of 'The Crow and the Cunning Fox'.

Activity Sheet

- Find the story of 'The Crow and the Cunning Fox' in a story book and read it to the children, as well as the description of the jars found at Lothal.
- Show them some pictures of Indus Valley ceramics.
- They should then imagine that they are an Indus artist from Lothal and draw their own versions of 'The Crow and the Cunning Fox', or another fable, on the outlines of the jar.

Developments

- The children could compare their versions of Indus Valley ceramic art with pictures of actual examples. How are they different? Why?
- They could use clay to make similar-shaped pots, use their designs and paint them on.
- They could investigate the ceramic art of the Ancient Greeks. What is depicted on their pottery? Are there any similarities with the Indus Valley pottery?

	Ancient Greece	Indus Valley
Colours	Orange/black	Black/red/brown
Size	All sizes	All sizes
Subjects	Heroes, myths	Animals, stories

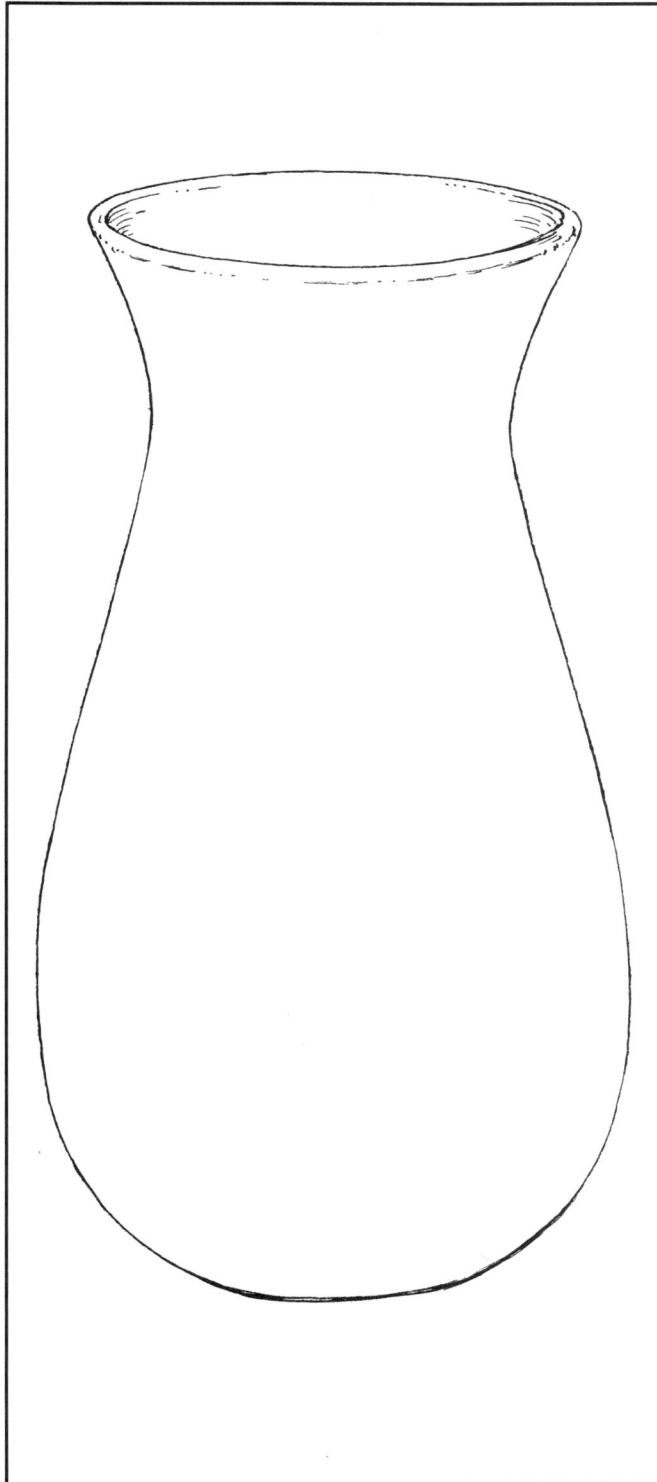

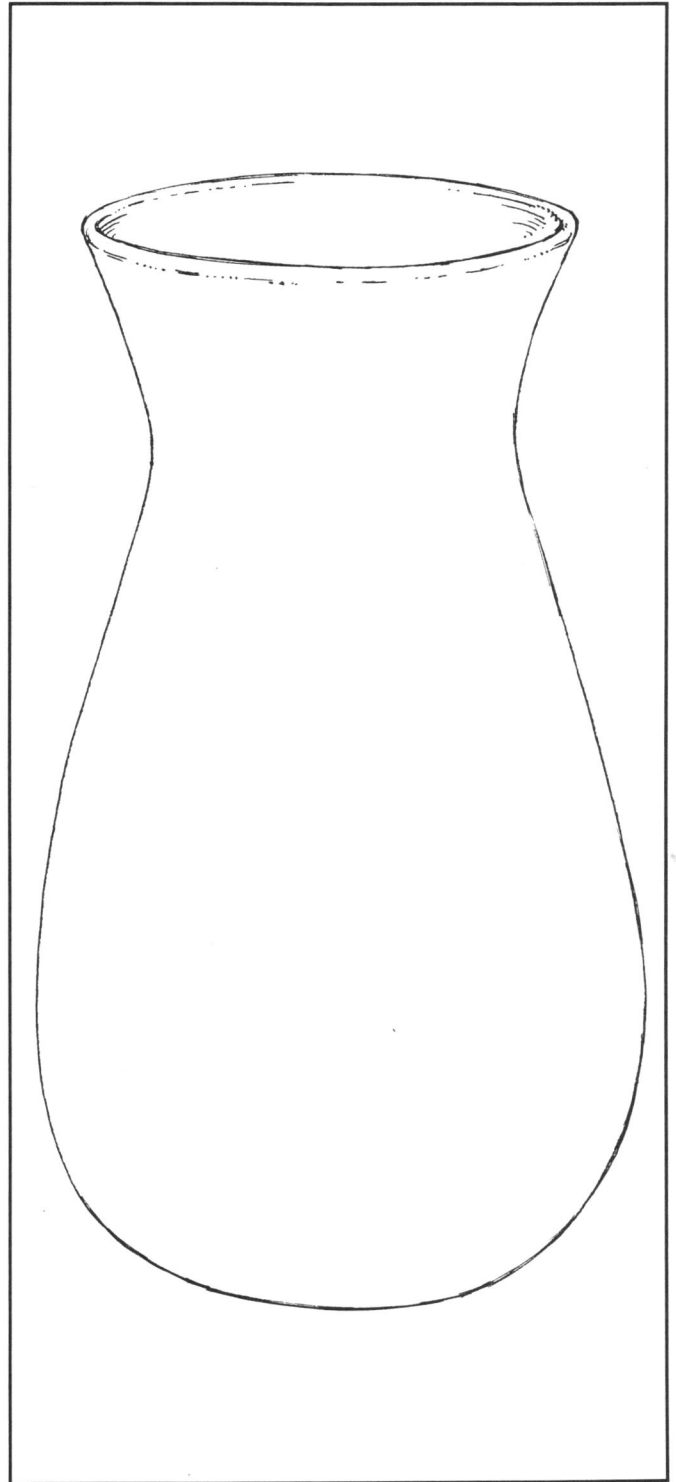

Ceramic art

- Decorate the jar outlines with pictures that tell a story or fable.
- Use colours the Lothal artist might have used.

view 1

view 2

Bead making –

Aims

- To introduce children to a technique, developed in the Indus Valley, which has not been improved in 4000 years.
- To discuss issues of the legacy of the Indus Valley civilisation.

ANCIENT INDUS BEADS   MODERN INDIAN BEADS

Activity Sheet

- Talk with the children about the kinds of stones used to make beads, for example:
  – agate
  – carnelian
  – onyx.
  If possible have examples of the minerals and/or stones, or items of jewellery in which the stones have been used.
- Working in twos, the children could cut and sequence the bead-making instructions. When they are happy with the order, they should paste the strips on to a sheet of paper and discuss their results with another group.

Background

Lothal's chief commercial activity was making and trading beads made from a variety of materials such as copper, shell and gemstones.

Even today the bead makers of Cambay (in the Indian state of Gujarat), who export all over the world, use the same technique that was developed by the bead makers of Lothal thousands of years ago.

The correct order of the sequence for making beads is as follows: put the stones into an earthen bowl to be cooked; remove the outside of the stone; split the stone to size with a hammer; shape the stone; rub one stone against another; polish the stone in a leather rotary drum; drill each bead with a double-edged drill; re-heat the beads if they are required in a deeper colour.

Developments

- The children could try making pictorial representations of each stage in the process. In this case the strips could be used to caption each illustration.
- Make a collection of beads of all kinds. What different materials are they made from? Could all these materials have been used by the Lothal bead-makers? Which ones definitely could not?

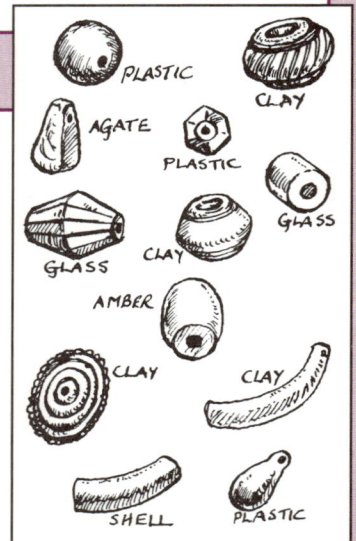

Made from?	Indus Valley?	Why?
Plastic	No	Not invented yet
Agate	Perhaps	A natural stone
Amber	Perhaps	A natural stone
Clay	Yes	They had lots of clay
Glass	No	No evidence of glass

- Ask the children to draw up a list of skills required to make beads in Lothal. Where could the craftsmen have learned these skills? Were they passed on through families? Were they learned by individuals? Is there any evidence?
- Ask the children to draw and describe a day in the life of a bead maker for a class display.

Polishing
Drilling
Sanding down
Using a kiln
Shaping

Bead making

- Cut out the instructions. Put them in the right order so that an apprentice bead maker could follow the process.

To polish – place the smoothed stones in a leather rotary drum filled with grit.	If beads are required in a deeper colour, heat them again in a kiln and sand them down.
Drill each bead with a double-edged drill placed with point towards centre of bead.	Rub one stone against another to smooth their surface.
To get the size you need, split the stone by hitting it with a hammer.	Put the stones to be turned into beads in an earthen bowl filled with sawdust. Cook them in a kiln. This makes the outer layer soft enough to work.
Remove the outside of the stone by knocking it gently with a hammer made from animal horn.	Hold the stone between your fingers against a pointed bronze rod. Shape the stones by using pressure.

Indus crafts – Ideas Page

Aim

- To develop the understanding of continuity and change by investigating the use of different materials over time.

Activity Sheet

- Share the background information with the children or ask them to research materials used in making jewellery, then and now. You could make a classroom display of pictures of the different materials used and the objects made from them.
- The children could then select and mark the things that were used by Lothal craftspeople. Can they say what each was used for?

Background

Beads of gold and jasper that were found at Lothal resemble the pendants still worn today in plaits of hair on the forehead by women in Gujarat.

Also found at the site are: a gold ear stud and conical foils of gold with loop rings used as earrings; heart-shaped ornaments of soapstone; 21 bangles, some hollow and some solid. The poor people had bangles of shell and terracotta. Other beads found at Lothal include those made from steatite (chlorite), some of which are carved with a trefoil design and are thought to have been of religious significance. Beads made from copper, gemstones (such as carnelian, jasper and agate), shell, ivory, bone and clay, were also found.

The abundant supply of metals was another factor contributing to the urbanisation of Indus settlements. Copper was used for making arrowheads, spearheads, fish-hooks, chisels, drills, tools and ornaments, as well as for jewellery.

Lothal was an important centre where shell working took place. Half-finished and completed artefacts of ivory, such as combs, rods and boxes have also been found at a workshop on the site.

Developments

- Jewellery was very popular with the Indus Valley people. How might items of jewellery have been traded among the local people?
- Set up a market for Indus artefacts such as jewellery, pots and utensils. The children could make examples of each based on pictures they have researched.
- Ask them to research where the raw materials for some of the crafts came from. Is there evidence to support any theories they might have? They could record their research on a chart such as the one below.

Material	My idea about where it came from	Reason	Evidence
Gold	From the north	Gold in mountains	None
Clay	River Indus	Local	Clay analysed
Shell	The Arabian sea	Local	Shells still nearby
Copper	From south India	None locally	None
Ivory	From south India	None locally	None

- How valuable do the children think these materials were? Would ivory be more valuable than clay? Why?
- They could think of other materials that we use today, that the Lothal people did not.

26   IDEAS BANK – *The Indus Valley*   © Folens

Indus crafts

● Tick those things that the Indus people used in their crafts.

clay	pencils	nylon
plastic	gold	shell
bone	carnelian	terracotta
sawdust	steel	copper
ivory	polystyrene	soapstone
rayon	bronze	fur

NOW ● Why did the Indus people not use some of these items?

Aim

- To encourage the children to understand the use of archaeological evidence as clues to aspects of everyday life.

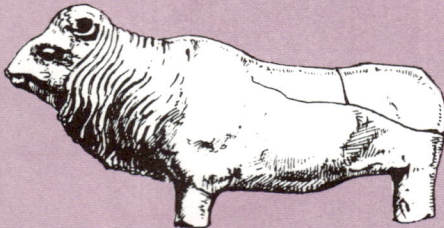

Activity Sheet

- Ask the children to study the pictures on the activity sheet.
- In pairs or small groups, they could discuss what they see and write down the things that they can deduce from the pictures.
- Later the whole class could discuss what each group has put on their chart. Are there differences? Why should this be?
- What evidence would they need to give them a clearer indication?

Background

In addition to dice and chess pieces, a number of other terracotta figures were found at Lothal and other sites. A few represented human beings and these were very realistic. One bust of a male had slit eyes, a sharp nose and a square-cut beard and is similar to stone sculptures found at Mari (in what was Mesopotamia). Another figure was of an Egyptian mummy with incised mouth and eyes and a pinched-up nose. Several female figures were also found.

Animal figures include lifelike representations of the ram, the rhinoceros, the humpless bull and the horse. Some animal figures had wheels and movable heads, suggesting that they were used as toys. Models of modes of transport include two kinds of carts (one with a solid chassis, one with a perforated chassis) and a model of a ship with provision for a mast and a sail.

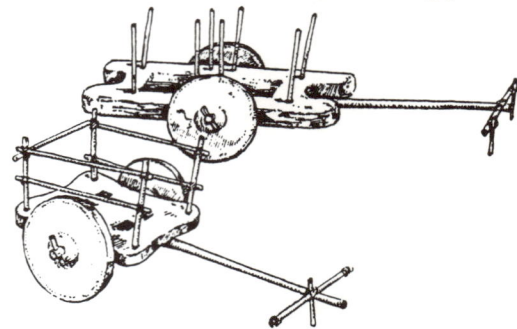

Cylindrical perforated jars have been found at several Indus sites. Archaeologists are still debating their use.

Developments

- After the class as a whole has discussed everyone's conclusions, the results could be discussed and finally entered on to a class chart.

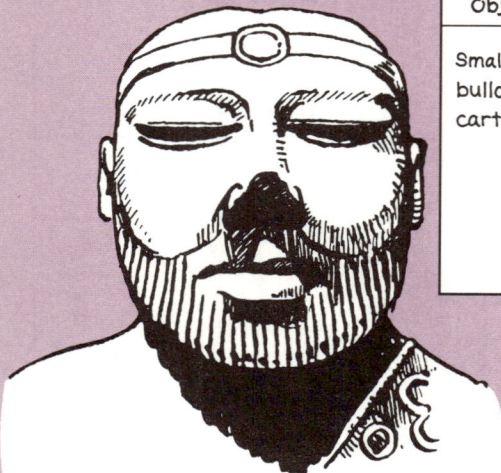

Objects	Our deductions	Evidence
Small clay bullock carts	Indus people used terracotta to make toys. They played with games and toys. Bullock carts were used as land transport.	Made from clay. Other toys on the sheet. They made toys of what they knew.
	Wheels were used to make transport easier. The Indus people bred animals and trained them for their own purposes.	Carts have wheels. Oxen need to be trained.

- Ask the children to write five questions they would like to have answered about the objects on the sheet. Where might they find the answers? Which answers are not available? Why?

Learning from artefacts

- Look at the drawings below. They are of objects that have been found at archaeological digs at Lothal and other Indus Valley sites.

- What can you find out about these artefacts?

- Complete a chart such as the one below with your findings.

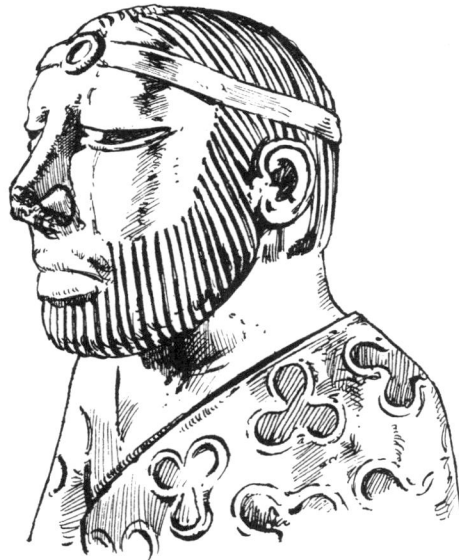

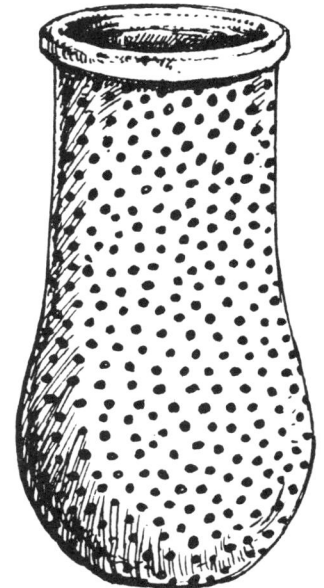

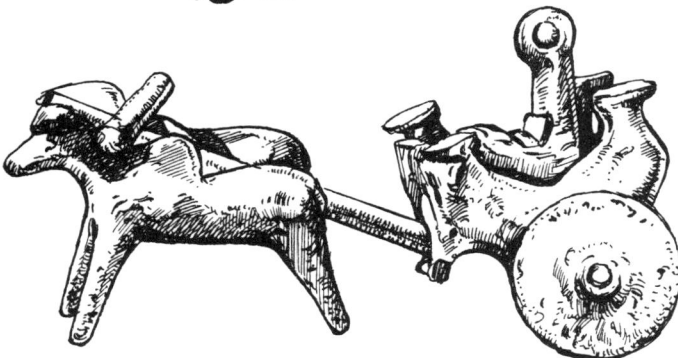

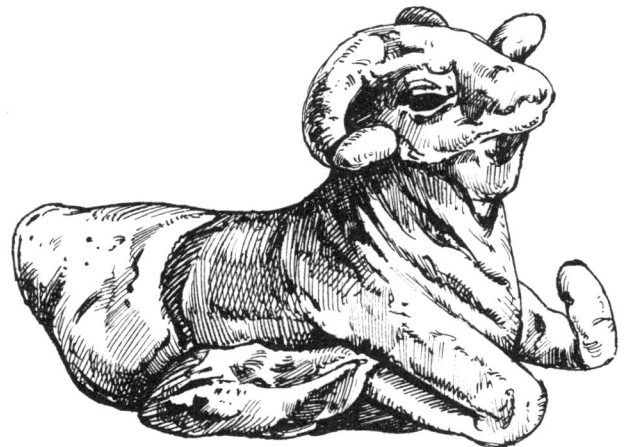

Object	Made from?	How made?	Possible use?
Bust of man	limestone	by hand	ornament

Linear measure – Ideas Page

Aims

- To show the children the accuracy achieved in measuring units of length.
- To demonstrate that the Indus Valley Civilisation had an advanced linear measuring system.

Background

Three scales, one each from Mohenjo-daro, Harappa and Lothal, have been discovered. These formed the basis of linear measurements in the Indus civilisation and are all integrated. The ivory scale from Lothal has decimal divisions which are the smallest so far known in the Indus civilisation. The available length of the scale is 128mm but only 27 graduations can be seen over a length of 46mm. The rest have worn off. The average distance between graduation lines is 1.704mm. The sixth and twenty-first graduation lines are longer than the rest, although no-one is sure why. The scale is 15mm wide. The very small graduations suggest that the Lothal scale was used for finer measurements.

Activity Sheet

- Ask the children to read the information given on the activity sheet and then attempt to make a scale similar to those used by Lothal citizens. Make sure that they understand that the real Lothal unit was approximately 1.7 mm and not the 2mm shown on the activity sheet to make the calculations easier.
- Ask the children to use the scale they have made to measure the objects listed on the table and to compare the results with the metric equivalent.

Developments

- Can the children think of any problems that might arise when a society such as that of the Indus peoples uses more than one system of measurement? Can any parallels be drawn with recent times?
- Discuss with the children why a civilisation should need a measuring system and what uses would be made of it. What would need to be measured and why? They could brainstorm their ideas.

A measuring system helps with ...	Implications
making regular-sized bricks	Buildings easier to build and stay up longer
making straight, even roads	Quicker and easier to travel and to trade
making larger buildings	Buildings last longer, quicker to build, can be stronger

- Compare the Indus scale with the scale of the Ancient Egyptians. Which might be considered more accurate by today's standards?

Civilisation	Name of measurement	Length
Ancient Egypt	Cubit	From the elbow to the tip of the longest finger.
Indus Valley	'Lothal'	Lothal unit = 1.7 mm.

Measurement

An ivory measuring instrument, used to measure length,
was found at Lothal. The units were marked.
This showed that the people of the Indus Valley had a standard
measuring scale. We do not know what they called the units.

- Make a ruler with a Lothal scale.
- Give a name to the units.
- Use this ruler to measure objects in your classroom.
- Complete the chart.

The Lothal scale

Object	Lothal scale	Metric scale
table		
door		
window		
bookshelf		
sink		
pencil		
book		

- List the sort of things that the Lothal people
  might have measured with this scale.

Religion – Ideas Page

Aims

- To draw inferences relating to the religious practices of the Indus people from the archaeological finds.
- To look for possible links between the Hindu religion and the religion of the Indus people, by examining evidence.

Activity Sheet

Provide: pictures of Hindu deities (see page 47).

- Share and discuss the background information with the children.
- Pairs of children could read the statements on the activity sheet and join them to the appropriate pictures.
- Working in pairs, the children could look at the seal and the statue of the 'Mother Goddess', as well as the pictures on the activity sheet and the Hindu deities shown on page 47. What can they see? What does the seal suggest about the religious practices of the Indus people?
- The children may link the Hindu religion to the seal or the 'Mother Goddess'. The final question should show them that while the evidence is interesting, there is no conclusive evidence linking modern Hinduism to the religion of the Indus people. Some historians do not believe that the two are related.

Background

Comparatively little is known about the religious beliefs of the Indus people. Without written records we will not know for certain what they believed or how they worshipped, but remains found at the main sites do offer clues:

- Seals appear to depict religious scenes. Some show a horned figure. One has a three-faced God surrounded by animals; this is thought to be a prototype of Pasupathi (Shiva, lord of beasts). One shows a sacrifice.
- Terracotta figures of a female have been discovered at many Indus sites but not Lothal. She is often called a 'Mother Goddess'.
- Fire altars have been found in houses and public places at Lothal and Kalibangan. This suggests that the Indus citizens worshipped a fire god. The horned deity shown on three seals (under an arch of flame) can be linked to the fire god, Agni.
- Brick-built altars containing animal bones have been found at Lothal and Kalibangan.
- The Great Bath found in the citadel at Mohenjo-daro may have been used for a religious or ritual purpose (see page 14). This compares with ritual tanks – pushkara – found adjoining Hindu temples even now. The steps may be compared to the ghats, characteristic of many Hindu pilgrimage places.
- Statues of painted bulls have been found at some sites.

Developments

- What do individuals understand by the term 'Mother Goddess'?
- What gifts do they think a 'Mother Goddess' might bring to the people who prayed to her – in Indus Valley times? – now?
- Can the children draw any other parallels between the Hindu religion and that of the Indus people from what they have learned?
- The children could research the elements of Hindu religious practice outlined on the activity sheet.

Religion

- Read these statements about the Hindu religion today. Join them to the appropriate pictures.

| Some deities are shown as female. | Bathing is an important part of the Hindu religion. | Hindu deities are associated with different animals. |

| The cow is sacred to Hindus. | Hindus use lighted diva lamps in their worship. |

| Shiva is often shown sitting cross-legged and thinking. | Hindus have sacred symbols such as 'Om' and the swastika. |

- Look at these two Indus artefacts. Is there enough evidence to link the Hindu religion to the religion of the Indus people?

IDEAS BANK – *The Indus Valley*

Aim

- To show how archaeological evidence can help in making deductions about the past.

Background

A number of cemeteries have been excavated at Indus sites. At Lothal, some graves which have been dated between 2200 and 2000BC contained two human skeletons, one male and one female. This suggests immolation of the wife at her husband's death. It may correspond to the now illegal Hindu practice, Sati, where a wife throws herself on to her husband's funeral pyre (thus being thought to 'attain virtue'). No joint burials have been unearthed which date after 2000BC.

The bone and horn of a goat found in two graves suggest the offering of a goat for the dead person. References to such offerings are found in the ancient sacred text, the *Satapatha Brahmana*: the animal is offered to Agni, the fire god, to carry the dead one safely to the next world. The estimated population of Lothal was 15 000 but only 17 skeletons have been found. This suggests that cremation was also practised.

Activity Sheet

- Introduce the activity by reading aloud the information from the activity sheet.
- The children could then read and discuss the information in pairs or small groups.
- They could highlight or underline the key ideas. Can the children identify where a point of view is being expressed?
- Pairs of children could discuss each statement and mark the sheet having decided on reasons for their answers.

Developments

- Discuss the possible significance and interpretations of male and female bodies being found in the same grave.
- Children could investigate and compare death rites of other ancient civilisations with those of the Indus people.

Rite	Indus Valley	Ancient Egypt
The body	Skeletons found	Mummified
Burial	Buried in grave	Buried in tomb
Grave goods	Some possessions left	Possessions left
Ritual	Sacrifice for the next world	Book of the Dead for the next world

- What are the similarities and differences between funeral rites of the Indus people and those practised in India or Pakistan today?
- Visit a graveyard or crematorium. What can children learn about the people buried there from the monuments and inscriptions?

Evidence	What I noticed	Deduction
Size	It is a very large marble tomb	A rich, important family
Dates	1788–1811	Died young
Inscription	Mentions sacrifice to country and war	Killed in the war?

Death rites

- Read about what was found in cemeteries at Lothal, Harappa and Kalibangan. Complete the chart.

The cemeteries contain a number of human skeletons. Those found at Lothal suggest a system where two people are buried together. Two of the three graves contained two human skeletons – a male and a female. This practice was given up by 2000BC. No joint burials were found after this time. In the single burials unearthed, dating from after 2000BC, the simple pit containing the body also contained some bowls, jars and a dish on a stand. Sometimes a shell bead or carnelian bead was put into a grave. Only seventeen skeletons have been found at Lothal, though the population was thought to be as large as 15 000. On one skeleton a copper earring was found. A bone and a horn of a goat were found in two graves.

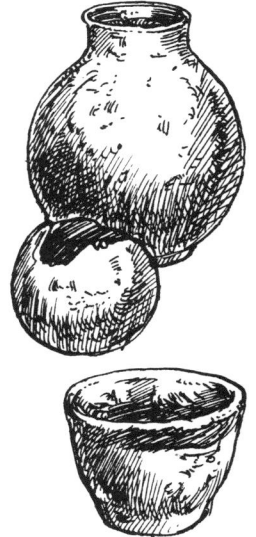

Statement	unlikely	likely	evidence
Some graves contained more than one body.			
Husbands and wives were sometimes buried together before 2000BC.			
Dead people were sometimes cremated.			
Jewellery was not always removed when people were buried.			
Animal offerings were sometimes made at burials.			
Only seventeen people died at Lothal.			
Bowls and jars were used in burial rites.			
The Indus people built elaborate tombs.			

Aims

- To discuss the notion that Lothal citizens had time to spare in their everyday lives.
- To introduce one of the items used at play.

Background

It is thought that the citizens of Lothal played a number of games. Evidence for thinking this is provided by:
- A complete set of games pieces similar to chess pieces. These pieces include animal figures, castle-like pieces and pyramids with an ivory handle. These are similar to those of the chess-set of Queen Hatshepsut in Egypt (1503–1482BC).
- Small dice. These are marked differently from the ones used today and those found at other Indus sites.

Activity Sheet

- Ask the children to make a Lothal dice and a modern dice using the nets provided.
- They should investigate the pairs of numbers on opposite faces of each dice. What do they find?
- They could suggest how the dice might have been used and by whom.

Developments

- In pairs, the children could invent a game which uses Lothal dice. They should write a set of instructions for other players. The game could then be tried by another pair or small group (depending on the nature of the game invented).
- Look at probability. Does the Lothal dice design result in different outcomes of probability?
- Does the discovery of dice suggest that the Indus peoples had time for play as well as work?
- The children could devise some questions that they would like to know the answers to in connection with leisure pursuits and games of the Indus people.

How were the dice made?

Who made them?

Who were they made for?

How did people play with them?

What did they need to know to make them?

- Many stones have been found which were used like marbles. Ask the children to list all the games they know that are played with marbles. Could they invent a new game?
- They could research whether such games are still played today in India.

Dice

Dice found at Lothal were marked in the following way:
1 opposite 2, 3 opposite 4, 5 opposite 6.
Modern dice are marked differently. Find a dice and look at it.
What do you notice about the pairs of numbers?

- Using the two nets make a Lothal dice and a modern dice.

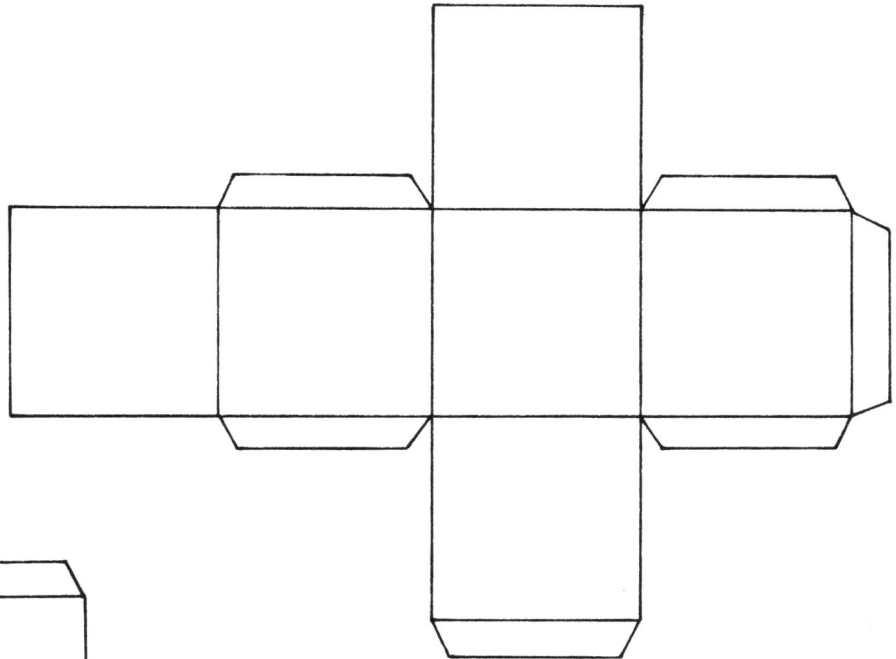

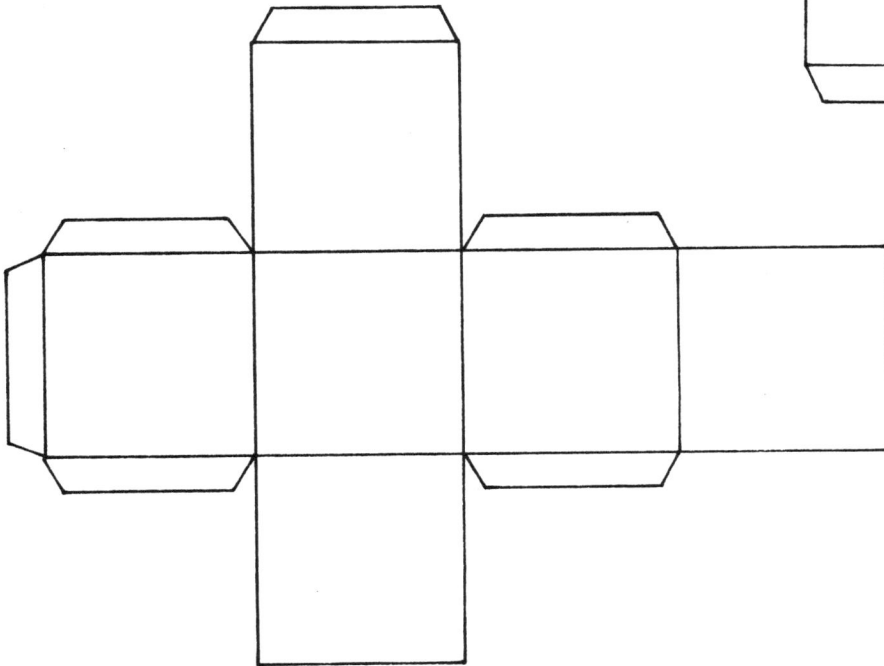

Devise a game that uses the Lothal dice. Can you use both a Lothal dice and a modern dice to play the same game?

Seals – Ideas Page

Aims

- To introduce the idea that Indus citizens used inscriptions and pictures as forms of communication or identification.
- To help children gain an appreciation of the level of artistic skill the Indus people had achieved.

Background

Seals have been found in all the important Indus sites. The characteristic seal helps archaeologists in determining whether a particular site belongs to the Indus civilisation or not. Most of the Indus inscriptions we have are on seals. Some seals, however, have been identified as being of Bahrein or Mesopotamian origin, indicating that trading took place between the civilisations.

   The precise function of seals is not certain but they are thought to have been used in trade and administration, possibly for stamping goods. Some archaeologists believe that they were tied to goods for trading and acted as labels.

Activity Sheet

- It would be useful to have an example of soapstone for the children to handle.
- Ask them to look at the illustration of the seals and the examples of the script. They could practise copying the examples of the signs.
- Can they suggest what any of them might represent?
- After reading the information they could then draw their own seal.
- They should then draw a seal that could not be from the Indus Valley, for example a picture of an aeroplane with writing in English.

Developments

- Can the children suggest what seals might have been used for?
- Explain that most of the seals have a boss at the back with a hole through it. How does this help to determine their use?

Evidence	Deduction
A boss with a hole in the back of the seals.	To feed a piece of rope or cord through. To tie on to something. To hang around the neck.

- What kind of tools might have been used to make the seals? What could the tools have been made from? What shape would they have been? Ask the children to draw and design an appropriate tool or tools.
- They could make a seal from modelling clay or plaster of Paris. Point out that the design is indented and not raised.
- Give each child a role-play situation, for example he or she is a merchant. The seal should show the goods being sold and how they are transported.

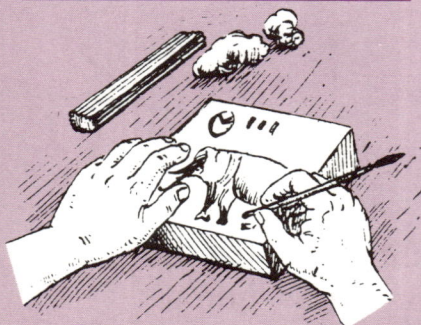

Seals

- Use the information and pictures of seals below, with the examples of Indus script, to design and draw two seals of your own:
  - one that could have been found in the Indus Valley.
  - one that could be found today.

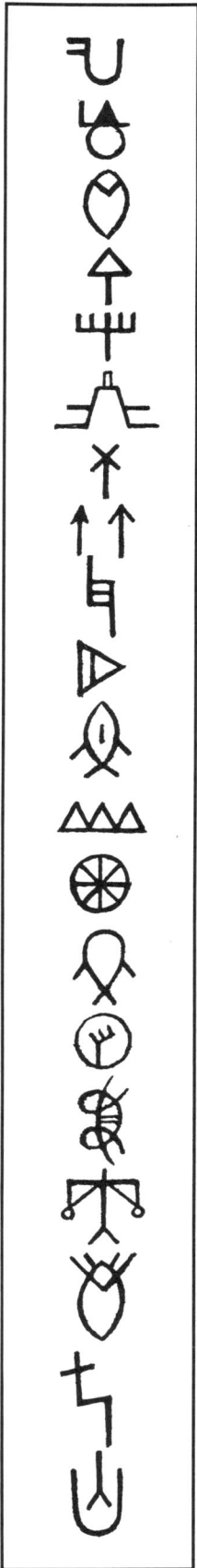

Over 2000 small rectangular objects made from soapstone (like those shown above) have been dug up by people excavating Indus Valley sites. These objects are known as seals and they are important archaeological evidence. No-one knows exactly what they were used for. The size of a seal ranges from 1x0.5cm to 6x6cm but the most common size was 3x3cm. Each seal has a picture and an inscription which uses symbols from the Indus script. Some examples of that script are shown on the right-hand side of this page. There are pictures of animals such as the humped bull, rhinoceros and water buffalo, as well as the tiger, elephant, mountain goat and a mythical three-headed creature. The most common picture is of the unicorn.

Aim

- To help children understand some of the difficulties in deciphering the Indus script.

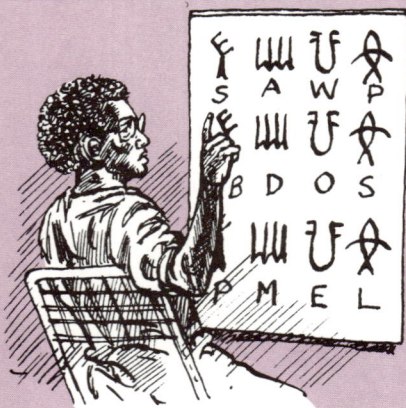

Activity Sheet

- Read and discuss the background information with the children.
- The children should then read the statements on the activity sheet and working in pairs try to form their diamond.
- When each pair has completed the diamond, the class should come together and in pairs present their arrangement to the others, giving reasons for their order. They could debate which reasons are most important.

Background

The Indus people were highly literate. They left behind more than 2500 seals bearing inscriptions in a mixed writing of pictures and signs. In total about 3500 inscriptions have been found. No inscriptions have been found on monuments.

A few Indus citizens probably wrote on other materials too, but these must have been highly perishable. As most inscriptions are on seals they are very short, often only a single sign. The average number of signs in a text is less than five. The longest continuous text has seventeen signs in three consecutive lines. Most commonly a seal has a picture (usually an animal) and a short inscription.

So far there have been 42 published attempts at deciphering the Indus script. None of the claims agree on any solution. The main reasons for the difficulty in deciphering the script are:

- The length of the inscriptions.
- The number of signs – too large to be alphabetic and too small to be purely ideographic.
- No bilingual text has so far been discovered.
- The script does not appear to be related to any known script of the same period.

Computers are now used to collect, arrange and publish all known inscriptions and to analyse them.

Developments

- The children could produce some messages in code and discuss how codes can be deciphered.
- Present a short text in a language and alphabet unfamiliar to the class. What can the children discover about it? They could plan an investigation.

Questions to investigate	Discoveries
How frequently does a sign occur in the text? How many times is it found in the first position? How many times in a second? Which pairs of signs occur together frequently?	

- How does this procedure highlight the difficulties of deciphering the script?
- Research and find one scholar's version of some pictograms. Ask the children to use them in messages or to think of other meanings for the signs.

Writing

- Read these statements about why the Indus Valley script has not been understood.
- Cut them out. Form a diamond by placing the most important reason at the top, the next two most important reasons in the second row and so on, with the least important reason at the bottom.

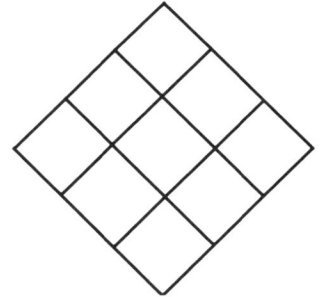

The sign list includes birds, fish, man, arrow and plain strokes

The average number of signs in a text is less than five

The writing does not appear to relate to any other writing of the same period

No writing has been found on monuments

Most inscriptions have only one line

The writing of the Indus people was very attractive

Indus citizens probably wrote on materials other than seals. This material was perishable

No inscriptions in two languages have been found

Only a few people could write

Decline and end – Ideas Page

Aims

- To present the children with the idea that there is no agreed reason for the ending of the Indus urban civilisation.
- To familiarise them with some of the reasons put forward to account for the ending of the urban phase of the Indus civilisation.

Background

Many theories have been put forward by historians and archaeologists for the decline (and collapse) of the Indus civilisation but none have been proved. Frequent flooding, increased soil salinity (making growth of crops difficult), epidemics and fatal diseases, climatic change, Aryan invasion, earthquakes, deforestation and erosion are some of the possible causes suggested.

However, it is now thought more likely that there was no abrupt collapse, rather that there was a decline which happened over a long period and the reasons varied in different areas of the civilisation. A series of natural disasters and other events may have gradually upset the delicate balance which held the urban civilisation together.

Activity Sheet

- Use page 46 as well.
- Materials needed: a large sheet of cardboard for each group to make the gameboard; coloured pens; glue; adhesive covering to laminate finished boards.
- Make a boardgame with 100 spaces. The size of each space is dictated by the size of the rectangles containing statements on the activity sheet. (More cards can be found on page 46.)
- The design of the board could include Indus writing, seals, terracotta artefacts or imaginary scenes.
- The children could use ordinary dice and counters or make use of such items as the Lothal dice (see page 37). They could make their own pieces, perhaps from clay, as imitations of Indus artefacts, to move around the board.
- The winner of the game is the last person to reach the final space on the board.

Developments

- Children could make their own cards for the game. They should decide on events in the history of the civilisation and write on the instructions to test if they realise that a circumstance may have a positive or negative effect.
- Ask them to summarise reasons for the decline of the civilisation.

Reason	Evidence
Flooding	Salt deposits in the soil.
Changing sea-level	Ports now inland.
Violence	Bodies found unburied
Earthquake	
Population growth – food runs out	

- The children will probably think that sudden disaster will be the best solution. However, it is important to their sense of causation that they realise that the decline of the civilisation would have taken place over a long period of time and could have been due to many causes.
- Once the game has been played a number of times, a temporary display could be made.

IDEAS BANK – *The Indus Valley*

The decline and end game – 1

People are not sure exactly what happened to the Indus Valley civilisation, but this game suggests some of the things that might have taken place.

- Make a board-game about the ending of the Indus civilisation at Lothal.
- You will need to design and make a game board with 100 sections (numbered 1 to 100).
- Each card on the printed sheets is a section on your game board.
  Read and cut out each one, then stick them on to the appropriate space on the board.
- Invent two more events that could have happened at Lothal. Decide where each could fit on the board and the outcome for a player who lands on those spaces.
- The winner of the game is the person who reaches the end section of the board last.

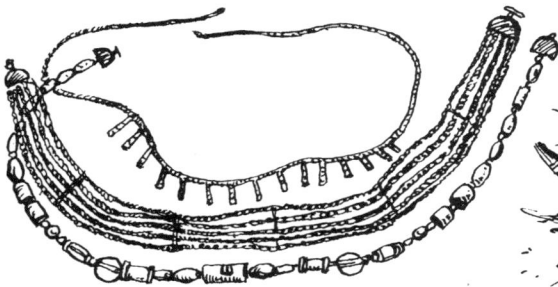

4 Bumper harvest. Grainstores overflowing. MISS 2 TURNS.	6 Trade with merchants in Mesopotamia good. Many people working as seal makers. GO BACK 1 SPACE.	10 Large import of gold jewellery. Necklace presented to Lothal. MISS 1 TURN.
11 Trees in hills felled to build more ships. MOVE ON 1 SPACE.	5 River flood lasts longer than usual. Part of town wall damaged. MOVE FORWARD 1 SPACE.	19 Town wall repaired. MISS A TURN.
22 Floods delay crop planting. Poor harvest. MOVE FORWARD 1 SPACE.	24 Large numbers of trees felled to fire brick kilns. MOVE ON 2 SPACES.	27 Ruler orders raising of platform level. MOVE BACK 1 SPACE.

Unanswered questions – Ideas Page

Aims

- To help children understand that there is still much to be discovered about the Indus civilisation.
- To encourage them to raise further questions.
- To realise that the lack of evidence may result in the answers never becoming clear.

Background

The undeciphered Indus script, the origins and the disappearance of the mature urban Indus civilisation are just three of the unsolved mysteries relating to the Indus people. There are many more questions still to be answered. For instance:

- How were the people governed? Was there a strong central authority like a ruler?
- Were there strict social classes?
- Did they have an army?
- What were their clothes like?
- What language did they speak?
- What did they look like?

Activity Sheet

- Draw the children's attention to the uncertainties about the decline of the Indus civilisation as indicated in the previous game.
- How complete is the picture we have of the Indus people and other aspects of their civilisation? Review with the children what they have learned and then ask them to use the activity sheet to write questions that still need answers.
- How can they attempt to find the answers to their questions?

Developments

- Make a survey of the answers to the final question on the activity sheet. What impact would a tiny piece of evidence have on the mysteries?

Mystery	Evidence needed
Where did the Indus people come from?	An ancient writer to tell us.
How were they governed?	Find a written law which names rulers.
Did they have an army?	Find some weapons and armour.
What did they wear?	Find some clothes or pictures of their clothes.

- Display the activity sheets in the class. Can any other children help in answering the questions or pointing the way to information sources or evidence?
- Compare the unanswered questions of other ancient civilisations to those of the Indus peoples. How far are the mysteries due to a lack of understanding of their written text?

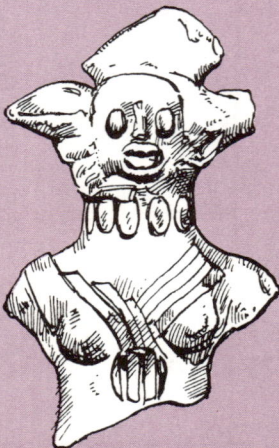

Unanswered questions

What do we still need to know about the Indus civilisation?
Write in the boxes what you think and if there is any evidence for your view.

Who were the Indus people? Where did they come from?	How were they governed?
Were there strict social classes?	Did they have an army?
What were their clothes like?	My question:

NOW What evidence would really need to be found to answer these questions?

The decline and end game – 2

- Read and cut out each card.
- Use the cards for 'The decline and end game' on page 43.

33 Major flood.
All people living outside town drowned.
HAVE ANOTHER THROW.

36 Large part of town wall washed away.
Lower town flooded.
MOVE FORWARD 3 SPACES.

37 Bead-makers stop work to rebuild houses.
Trade temporarily halted.
GO ON 2 SPACES.

40 Shortage of timber.
Very few fired bricks made.
MOVE ON 1 SPACE.

45 Continuous rains flood town.
Drains overflow into streets.
HAVE ANOTHER TURN.

48 No fuel (wood) to boil water or cook. Many in lower town die in epidemic.
FORWARD 2 SPACES.

53 Fleet of trading ships fails to return.
MOVE ON 2 SPACES.

55 Earthquake in the Mohenjo-daro region.
Raw materials cut off.
Trade disrupted.
GO ON 3 SPACES.

59 Townspeople spend more time searching for food, water and wool.
THROW DICE AGAIN.

61 Not enough fodder for buffalos.
Numbers decline.
MOVE FORWARD 1 SPACE.

64 Fishing boats destroyed in storm.
Fish shortage.
GO ON 1 SPACE.

66 Lothal ruler and family fail to return from Harappa. Captured or killed by Aryan invaders?
HAVE 2 MORE THROWS.

67 Acropolis area taken over by ordinary townspeople to get away from floods.
MOVE ON 1 SPACE.

72 Merchants build factory and employ remaining bead craftsmen.
GO BACK 1 SPACE.

73 River changes course.
Boats stranded in dock.
MOVE ON 3 SPACES.

75 Merchant organises working parties to re-open dock.
MOVE BACK 2 SPACES.

81 Salt water floods fields. Crops fail again.
FORWARD 2 SPACES.

88 Major flood. Many drowned.
TAKE 2 EXTRA TURNS.

100 Last people leave Lothal for safety of higher ground.

IDEAS BANK – *The Indus Valley*

Hindu deities

BRAHMA

VISHNU

SARASVATI

LAKSMI

SHIVA

GANESHA

DURGA

Eight ways to help ...

There are hundreds of ideas in this book to enable you to develop and extend the photocopiable pages. Here are just eight ways to help you make the most of the Ideas Bank series.

1 Photocopy a page, paste on to card and laminate/cover with sticky-backed plastic to use with groups. Children can now write on the pages using water-based pens and this can be washed off.

2 Photocopy on to both sides of the paper. Put another useful activity on the back. Develop a simple filing system so others can find relevant sheets and do not duplicate them again.

3 Save the sheets – if the children do not have to cut them up as a part of the activity – and re-use. Label the sets and keep them safely in files.

4 Make the most of group work. Children working in small groups need one sheet to discuss between them.

5 Put the sheets inside clear plastic wallets. This means the sheets are easily stored in a binder and will last longer. Children's writing can again be wiped away.

6 Use as an ideas page for yourself. Discuss issues with the class and get children to produce artwork and writing.

7 Make an overhead transparency of the page. You and your colleagues can now use the idea time and time again.

8 Ask yourself, 'Does every child in this class/group need to deal with/work through this photocopiable sheet?' If not, don't photocopy it!

IDEAS BANK – *The Indus Valley*